Tao Seeker

The Quest for Infinite Wisdom

AMIT BASU

Tao Sutra

The Quest for Infinite Wisdom

All content and photographs copyright © 2014 Amit Basu

ISBN: 978-1-941474-00-6

Amit Basu asserts the moral right to be identified as the author of this work.

This book is entirely a work of fiction. The names, characters and incidents portrayed in it are the work of the author's imagination. Any resemblance to actual persons, living or dead, events or localities is entirely coincidental.

All rights reserved. No part of this publication may be reproduced, stored in a retrieval system, or transmitted, in any form or by any means, electronic, mechanical, photocopying, recording or otherwise, without the prior permission of the publisher.

For further information, contact the publisher at:

Foobarzen Press

www.amitbasu.com

Printed in a far corner of the Universe.

To my family and friends.
This book would not have been possible without you.

Tao 1:1 - The Ripple

"What is the purpose of life, O Tao?" asked the student who was sitting quiet for a long time.

"The purpose of life is to cause a ripple," said the Tao.

"Please explain, O Tao," said the student.

"The universe is a giant lake, and you are a pebble that hits its surface one day. You will eventually sink to the bottom without a trace; what will remain for a short time is the ripple that you created on the lake surface. So, go ahead, make a ripple! May be the ripple you make will touch another, and change it, which in turn will affect another one. So that, long after you are gone, the changes you have wrought may still be around," said the Tao.

The Tao paused. Then he added, "That, my son, is the purpose of life."

"Where is your ripple, O Tao?" asked the student.

"I am still gathering speed before I hit the surface," said the Tao.

Tao 1:2 – A Short but Intense Life

"Today's lesson is a story," said the Tao, "It is a story of colorful flags that were fluttering on a line above the high desert. It was a beautiful summer's day. The sky was bright blue, the wind was strong, the flags were flying high. They were feeling rather happy, and a few of them said, 'Look at us! We have such a charmed life. Living in this wonderful place, freely fluttering in the breeze, radiating the joy all the way up to the heavens. It does not get much better than this!' But there was a blue flag in the corner who did not share this emotion. She said, 'Yes, it is beautiful here. But do you see that your freedom is an illusion? That you are tied to the ground?' The red flag in the middle sneered, 'Well, if you do not like it here, why don't you leave?' 'Yes, I would love to let go, I would love to fly away if you would only help me cut loose,' the blue flag said. So they did, and she flew away, free as the wind."

"What happened, then?" asked a student.

"The answer depends on who you are," said the Tao.

"Tell us, O Tao," the student implored.

"The flags on the line sighed collectively, 'That is the end of her'."

"And the blue flag? What did she say?"

"The blue flag joyously said, 'Hurrah to new beginnings,' as she flew away."

"End of story?" asked the student, clearly wanting more.

"Almost ," said the Tao, " ... years later, an obituary appeared in a newspaper in a distant exotic land. 'She lived a short but intense life,' it said."

Tao 1:3 - Time

The Tao was admiring his new iWatch, for which he had stood in a long winding line under frigid rain outside the Apple Store.

"Why does this watch not show time?" asked the student.

"Because it is not a watch," said the Tao, "... and, anyway, measuring time is so passé ... how does it matter what time it is when time has neither beginning, nor end? All that matters is 'now', the moment you are in. And that moment is forever changing, so why even try to capture it? A watch is a symbol of man's futile exercise to bracket time to fit within his own meager understanding of the universe."

The student was taken aback at this passionate outpouring of wisdom. "But, what if you really want to know what time is 'now'?" persisted the student.

"There is an app for that," said the Tao.

Tao 1:4 - I'mperfect

"I feel so horribly imperfect," wailed the student one morning.

"And why would that be?" asked the Tao, curious.

"Everyone else is so perfect in every way: they have perfect lives, perfect friends and family, perfect looks, and, why, they even have perfect children with perfect 4-point-oh GPA. I have none of those. What should I do with my imperfect life, O Tao?"

"Are you sure that everyone but you is perfect?"

"Everyone but me! I can see it in their eyes, when they look at me. She is so imperfect, their eyes seem to say."

"If they are all perfect, does it not make the perfect ordinary?" pondered the Tao.

"How so?" asked the student.

"They all are so like one another. They all have their perfect lives that are made from the same mold. They always have the same routine: the Monday morning blues, the Tuesday evening helping the children with homework, the Wednesday making dinner, the Thursday evening washing clothes, the too-tired-to-make-love Friday nights, the Saturday Kumon classes, and the Sundays dreading the Mondays. That is perfect in your eyes, but it is really just uninteresting, ordinary life," said the Tao, waiting for his words to sink in.

Then he continued: "You, on the other hand, are imperfect and unique. Your days are filled with possibilities, your nights are adventurous sometimes, and feverishly creative at others. You live a different, unpredictable life that the perfect people wish they could. So, perhaps you should celebrate your imperfection!"

"I feel so gloriously imperfect," smiled the student one morning.

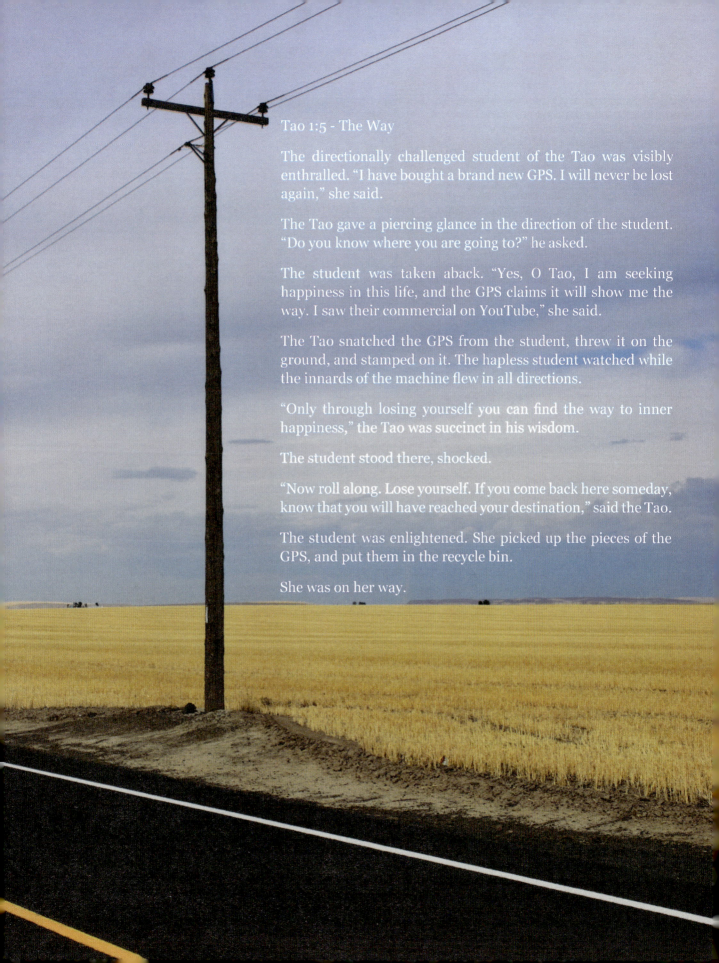

Tao 1:5 - The Way

The directionally challenged student of the Tao was visibly enthralled. "I have bought a brand new GPS. I will never be lost again," she said.

The Tao gave a piercing glance in the direction of the student. "Do you know where you are going to?" he asked.

The student was taken aback. "Yes, O Tao, I am seeking happiness in this life, and the GPS claims it will show me the way. I saw their commercial on YouTube," she said.

The Tao snatched the GPS from the student, threw it on the ground, and stamped on it. The hapless student watched while the innards of the machine flew in all directions.

"Only through losing yourself you can find the way to inner happiness," the Tao was succinct in his wisdom.

The student stood there, shocked.

"Now roll along. Lose yourself. If you come back here someday, know that you will have reached your destination," said the Tao.

The student was enlightened. She picked up the pieces of the GPS, and put them in the recycle bin.

She was on her way.

Tao 1:6 - The Past

The Tao was on a safari with the student. They were traveling in silence for over an hour when the student asked, "I always wonder what would have happened if I took a different path?"

"Look back," the Tao said, "What do you see?"

The student looked back. The late afternoon's golden sunlight was filtering through the dust raised by the Jeep they were traveling on. It was a wonderful sight.

"I see only dust," said the student.

"That is your past," said the Tao, "Looking back, it appears mysterious, beautiful, filled with possibilities. But, in reality, there is nothing to find there anymore, only the dust of your memories floating around. Let us move on, shall we?"

They travelled in silence for the next hour.

Tao 1:7 - The Walk of Life

It was late afternoon. The sun rays, filtering through the clouds, were golden. The Tao was on a hiking trail through the lonely mountains. He came across a woman on the trail. She had flowers in her hair. She wore running shoes.

"Hi! How are you doing?" said the Tao, in greeting.

"Doing great! Where are you going?" said the woman. With a gentle shake of her hair, the flower fell to the ground.

"Nowhere in particular," said the Tao, pausing in his step to pick up the flower.

"Why don't you walk with me?" asked the woman.

So they did. For many moons.

"We have been walking long together. Do you have the same destination as me?" asked the woman one day.

"No. Our destinations are different," said the Tao, "We only share the walk."

So they walked the Walk of Life. Together.

Tao 1:8 - Vision

"Isn't she a beauty?" the student asked the Tao. He was holding a Leica SXY camera.

"She is," said the Tao, "She is expensive, isn't she?"

"Very," said the student proudly, "She has a great, sinuous, sleek body. And a 337 megapixel sensor! Not to mention the vibration-inducing supersonic motor ultra-zoom pro-series f/0.1 lens. It is a great feeling to hold her in my hands! When I look through her eyes ..."

"What do you not see?" interrupted the Tao.

"What do you mean, O Tao?" the student was surprised, "I guess you mean what do I see?"

"What do you not see?" repeated the Tao.

Then, all of a sudden, the truth dawned on the student. He saw the meaning of Tao's wisdom. In the moment's excitement, the Leica slipped out of his hands and crashed to the floor. Broken glass flew in all directions.

A photographer was born that day.

Tao 1:9 - Life

The Tao was asked about the meaning of life. Thus he spoke:

"Your life is floating around in a multi-dimensional time-space-consciousness continuum. When you were born, the boundary conditions were set along the axis of time. But, space and consciousness dimensions are left unbounded, and for you to explore. That, which you explore, will be the meaning of your life."

The student bowed at the great wisdom, and, thus enlightened, turned to leave.

"Uh, and one more thing ... ," said the Tao.

The student turned, expectant.

"...the answer is not 42."

Tao 1:10 - Beautiful

"Make me beautiful," the prettiest of Tao's students asked the Tao.

"But you are beautiful," said the Tao.

"No. I am not. I am too fat. There are shadows on my face. My eyes look dazed. I hate my hips. My breasts are too big. I feel ugly," She was on the verge of tears.

"Ok. Let me see what I can do," said the Tao. He waved his hands around. There were smoke and mirrors. There were flashes of light, and the ugly shadows ran for cover. The Tao's voice, chanting "f2.8, 1/125, catch-light, depth-of-field", was heard above the din. She stood there, uneasy, unblinking, motionless, through all the drama.

When the smoke cleared, there she was. She was not fat. Her face glowed. The eyes sparkled. She loved her hips. Her breasts were just right. She felt beautiful.

"I feel beautiful," the student gushed, "Thank you, O Tao."

"Believe me, you are just the same," said the Tao, "What has changed is that now you also have a beautiful self-image."

"Whatever!" said the student, "Just do it again!"

Tao 1:11 – The Problem

"I have a problem," said the nerdy student.

"And what would that be?" the Tao was mildly curious.

"I have a social problem, or, rather, a problem with the society. I think no one likes me. No one likes my posts on Facebook. I post such wonderful stuff: links from the boundless abyss of the cyberspace, grainy iPhone photos, lolcat YouTube videos, smart and witty quotable quotes that someone else has curated from somewhere else. I spend hours and hours, logged onto Facebook, waiting for someone to click on my posts, someone to say she likes them, and may be write a comment or two. But, so far, nada! No one likes my posts. No one comments! I know, I know, that they are out there, hiding behind their computer screens, reading my wall for free. They are like the cheap tourists who gorge on free buffet. I am exasperated."

"Have you considered leaving Facebook?", asked the Tao, "May be you wont have this problem then?"

"I have thought about it, O Tao," said the student, "If I leave Facebook, I will not have my social problem. But … I wont have a society either."

"Houston, I think we have a diagnosis," muttered the Tao.

Tao 1:12 – A Matter of Perspective

The Tao was playing tennis with his student. "How do you play so well, O Tao?" asked the student, "You are so nimble. You are always able to get rid of the ball."

"I think of every ball as a gift of love that I am sending to you. I do not think of it as getting rid of the ball, but as sending my gift to you. The more gifts I give you, the better I feel," said the Tao.

"We think so differently, O Tao," said the student, "I was thinking of it as a evil-smelling bag of crap I need to send away from me."

"To win the game, your thinking is perhaps more effective," the Tao smiled, "but in my mind, I win every time."

Tao 1:13 - Knowledge

"I am afraid I have some bad news," said the Tao.

"No, please, not now, O Tao," said the student, half-drunk, "This is a party. The bad news can wait, can it not?"

The Tao nodded.

"Meanwhile, enjoy this fine wine, O Tao," said the wealthy student, "I bought this today. 1970 vintage Château Mont Blanc. Mighty expensive too, if I may add. It has fabulous aftertaste which you would not find in those cheap wines. See, the slight hint of garden-fresh strawberries of golden Mediterranean summer, and just a whiff of aged oak; I can almost feel I am transported to the French Riviera, for that ethereal smell of the virgin countryside has been bottled in here. To taste this is to get just that much closer to heaven."

"I am afraid I have some bad news," the Tao repeated.

"Ah, well, just tell us then, if you must," said the student.

"The 1970 vintage Château Mont Blanc bottle broke in the kitchen. This is a five dollar Chilean wine that I picked up from the local grocery store," said the Tao.

The student put down his wine glass hurriedly. "No wonder all the time I was thinking that the tannin just did not feel right."

Tao 1:14 - Wisdom

"What was there at the beginning, O Tao?" asked the curious student.

"At the beginning, the world was born anew. There was only wonder. But soon ... there was happiness, content and some ... pain," said the Tao.

"And then, in the middle?" asked the student.

"The middle was the most complex," pondered the Tao, "There was affection, love, hate, lust, jealousy, greed and anger. It was a strange cocktail of emotions. Wonder ebbed away. Sense of content diminished. Both happiness and pain reached extremes."

"And how did it end?" the student persisted.

"Content returned, even if in a small way," said the Tao, "But it was tinged with despair ..."

"I don't like how its progressing ... ," muttered the student.

"You haven't heard it all yet," said the Tao, "Then, before the end, there was a new beginning. The world was born anew. There was only wonder."

"Sounds like reincarnation," opined the student.

"No," said the Tao, "It is called wisdom."

Tao 1:15 – Shadows of the Mind

"I feel like a new man," said the Tao one morning, "A great realization has dawned on me last night."

"Tell us more," implored the student.

"It occurred to me when I was looking at the flickering oil lamp last night. While the lamp lit up the space around it, most of the shadows were underneath it. I realized that the light was the knowledge, and the shadow was my ego."

"What did you do to get rid of your ego?" asked the student.

"I decided that I must surround myself with people smarter than me, like you," the Tao said, "Always."

Tao 1:16 - Simplicity

"I don't understand you, O Tao," said the student, "You are so abstruse most of the time. Whatever you say, it is not always what it seems. I am so confused."

"Well, you should perhaps also smoke what I have been smoking," the Tao laughed.

"Huh?", the student was taken aback.

"Never mind. I will try to be add a dose of clarity to my lessons in future," said the Tao, "Now for today's lesson …"

There was hushed silence.

The Tao cleared his throat, and paused for effect.

"Understand complexity. Keep it simple," he said at last.

There was hushed silence.

"That will be all for today," said the Tao.

Tao 1:17 – Spring Forward, Fall Back

"Spring forward, fall back!" exclaimed the student during the morning lesson.

"It is that Daylight Savings Time again, I guess," said the Tao, looking none too pleased.

"Yes, and I have already moved forward all my watches and clocks."

"And how many do you own?" the Tao was inquisitive, for he had none.

"About seven that need to be changed. My watch, two wall-clocks, one clock each in the microwave oven and the cooking range. And two alarm clocks."

"And how long did it take?"

"I would say about ten minutes, since I had to bring down the wall-clocks," said the student.

"Well! Let us do some math today. So, if it took every household in USA five minutes to change the time in clocks today, how many total minutes of effort would that be?" asked the Tao.

"About 570 million minutes, or 9.5 million hours, or 395833 days, or 1084 years," the math wizard student's hand went up.

"If we paid minimum wage for changing time, it would translate to some 140 million dollars for the two time changes over a year," the Tao said, "So, what did we learn from this?"

"Abolishing Daylight Savings Time can possibly balance US budget," said the student, seriously.

"That too!" said the Tao, "But an evident proof of human being's intelligence is how unnecessarily complicated and wasteful a life we have created for ourselves."

"… Or how we are able to make complex and unintelligible deductions from simple numbers," muttered the student.

Tao 1:18 - Cool

"You are the coolest guy I have met, like ever!" the new student was all a-flutter after the class.

"And how is that?" the Tao wanted to know, for no one ever told him that he was cool.

"You are sooooooo cool. I heard you listening to Bieber, and did I tell you that I just loooove him! Come to think of it, you are perhaps a bit old, umm, but ... ok ... whatever! I was listening to you, like, and was thinking, wow, that dude sure knows some serious stuff, like he is talking of all these things that sound so like he has read them in a book or something ... I mean, you know stuff they don't even show on TV. And I totally dig your looks, like, retro and all. Seriously, it is a bit out of fashion, but you are in a niche. I mean, with your looks and smooth talking, you must be quite a Guru, like."

"Totally," the Tao smiled.

Tao 1:19- River

The Tao was on a boat on the Ganges. "Life is like a fast-flowing river," he said.

"Wouldn't that be just the right thing to say at this time?", smiled the student, "However … let us hear your pearl of wisdom anyway."

"Life is like a fast-flowing river which is so wide that you think you can barely see the shores. You are floating on it, bobbing up and down, and being carried by the stream of time. It is so fast that you can not swim upstream, try as you might. You can chalk out your own trajectory somewhat, but all the while it is pushing you downstream relentlessly."

"And what about the distant shores that I can not reach? What is there?" asked the student.

"Immortality," said the Tao.

Tao 1:20 - Possession

The Tao was polishing his Harley Davidson motorcycle. It was shining under the midday sun. The student stood there, admiring the beast of a machine.

"Why do you own a Harley, O Tao?" the student asked, "You have renounced most things in life, but not the Harley."

"It is a long story," said the Tao, "I had taken my first girlfriend out on this Harley."

"But you have renounced her," persisted the student.

"I renounced the Harley too, but when I came back, it was still there," the Tao said.

The student turned to leave. The Tao started the engine.

Tao 1:21 - Space

"Down there in the valley, the alphabet is in a state of turmoil," said the student, all excited.

"Go on," prodded the Tao, "Tell me more."

"The letters of the alphabet have taken against each other; each one wants its own space. The letter Z was the first to express its grievance. 'I have been relegated to the end, next to the filthy Y, don't know why,' it said, and moved away towards B. Soon M followed suit, muttering under her breath about how she had been living a miserable life, stuck in the middle, holding it all together; now she wants to break free, find some space to call her own. The numbers were on the warpath too, with 0 claiming how she was always made to feel like she did not count. Last I know, even 0x07 has lost it, complaining of a constant ringing inside her head. It is truly mayhem down there with everyone clamoring for space of their own, and the alphabet soup is about to boil," the student ended dramatically.

"I a m n o t s u r e i f s p a c e i s a l w a y s a g o o d t h i n g . Y o u m u s t u s e i t j u d i c i o u s l y t o g i v e m e a n i n g t o t o g e t h e r n e s s," said the Tao.

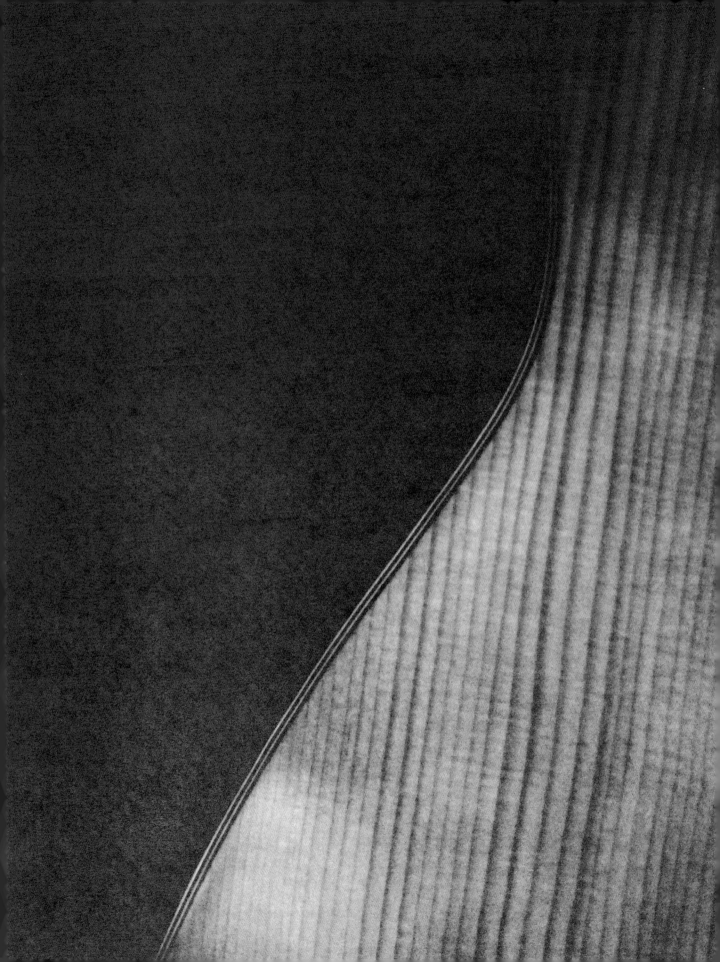

Tao 1:22 - Music

And so it was that the student, and Baul was his name, came in to the lesson with a guitar one day. "I would like to sing you a song, O Tao," he said, "I have written it myself."

"I would love to hear you," the Tao said, encouragingly, "Please go on."

The student sang a wonderful song, full of sweet melody that rose and fell like gentle waves driven by the evening sea breeze. The notes, and there were many of them, wafted on the air, looking for petals of the mind to gently sit on. The voice, enchanting and melancholy at the same time, communed with the soul. Through it all was the captivating sound of the guitar, that flowed effortlessly from his hand.

When it was over, there was silence. And then there was applause.

"Amazing," the Tao said, as the applause died down. And then: "You have reached your inner self and touched it with music. You do not need me any more. Go ahead and spread the harmony, with which you enthralled us today, among others. That would be your calling."

So the student left on his way.

And so it was.

Epilogue: Circa 2014. The student now lives comfortably in the suburbs. He caresses his Fender Stratocaster on Saturdays.

Tao 1:24 - Destination

"I feel I am nowhere I want to be," said the youth.

"None of us are, really," said the Tao. "Where do you want to be?"

"Nowhere else," said the student after a moment. "Where is it?"

"Guess on," pondered the Tao.

"So, what should I do?" asked the youth.

"Should you ever reach where you are, you will know,"
said the Tao.

Tao 1:23 - The Curious Dream of the Marathon Man

"I had this curious dream, O Tao! Please tell me what it means," the excited student spoke.

"Nothing! Dreams don't mean a thing!" said the Tao, unmoved.

"How could you say that, O Tao? I have not told you anything about the dream yet," said the puzzled student.

"Never mind. Go ahead, tell me about your dream," said the Tao.

"I was walking on a lonely desert. It was sizzling hot. I saw a figure at the distance, moving slowly, staggering, in a trance. As he came near, I saw he was thin, had a vacant gaze in his eyes; he had a earring in one ear. 'Dude! I have run out of water,' said the man, 'and I still have 185 miles more to go.' I took pity, and offered him some water. 'But where are you going? There is only desert for the next 500 miles that way,' said I. 'I will be turning back after 35 miles. Its a loop. I am running the Hellfire ultra-marathon,' said the man. 'Fool,' I thought under my breath, 'why would anybody be running in this heat?'. He looked at me carefully. 'Well, you are wearing the Hellfire t-shirt yourself. You must be running too?' asked he. 'Only in my dream,' said I. The man thought for a moment. Then he said: 'Funny that you say that. I had this curious dream. I was walking on a lonely desert. It was sizzling hot. I saw a figure at the distance ...' "

"Stop!" cried the Tao, "You are infected by the recursive Ultra-runner virus! No lessons today! Go, run a few miles. It will clear your mind."

Tao 1:24 - Destination

"I feel I am not where I want to be," said the student one morning.

"None of us are, really," said the Tao, "If we were where we wanted to be, where would we go from there?"

"Nowhere else," said the student after some thought, "Hmmm... that would be a boring life, won't it be?"

"Guess so," pondered the Tao.

"So, what should I do?" asked the student.

"Should you ever reach where you wanted to be, it is time to look ahead to find a new destination," said the Tao.

Tao 1:25 – Darkness and Light

"Are you afraid of the dark? Tell me true," asked the student one day.

"Yes, I am," said the Tao, "But that has not stopped me from stepping into the dark side within me. There is always a part of you that is in the shadows, that is where your hopes go to die. If you fear and stay away from your inner darkness, you never conquer it. It stays there, forever, looming larger, getting darker all the time. So, you must step into it, embrace it, and you will find that it is not as foreboding as it seems from the outside. After all, light and darkness are two sides of the same coin."

The student was enlightened.

He flipped the switch.

Tao 1:26 - Viewpoint

"Must we always keep moving on in life?" asked the student, "Is that the only way?"

"Yes," said the Tao, "However, seeking newer places is not enough; you must have new viewpoints too."

Tao 1:27 - Flight

"I always wanted to fly," said the student, "I heard that they are having discounted flying lessons at the Heaven's Gate Skyport."

"I wanted to be the wind," said the Tao.

"Nah!" said the student, "Flying sounds like an immensely more fun thing to do."

"Yes. But it is the wind that gives you wings."

Tao 1:28 - Change

"It is yet another day!" exclaimed the student, looking somewhat dejected, "Same old place, same old people, same old wisdom."

"You look unhappy," said the Tao, "The problem is not the place, or the people. The problem is inside you. The moment you say 'same old', you know you need a change. But, first, change yourself, even as you try to change the world around you."

Tao 1:29 - Future

"I can not see ahead, O Tao," said the student, "I don't know what is waiting for me. This thought frightens me. It creeps me out. I wish I could see the future through the fog of time."

"You can see your future, but only if you create your own," said the Tao.

Tao 1:30 – Journey

The student was riding his bicycle with the Tao up a hill, when he asked, "Where does this path end, O Tao?"

"End is an illusion," said the Tao, "But your journey, that is for real."

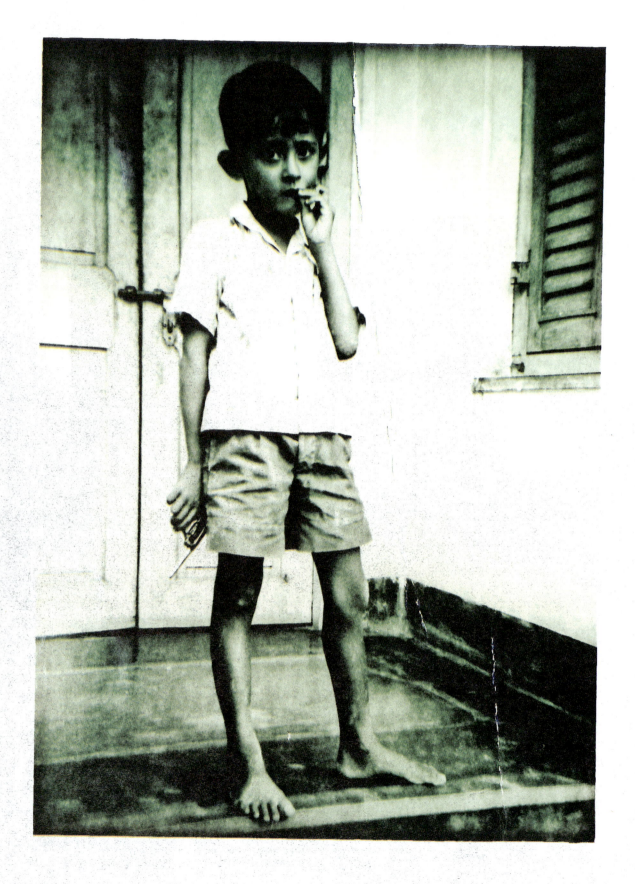

Tao 1:31 - Gun

"I bought a gun, O Tao, and registered with the NRA," said the student, "I feel so much safer now."

"Really? That should make me feel unsafe around you," the Tao laughed, "But pray, who are you afraid of?"

"There are weirdoes out there, O Tao. They are out to kill me. Don't know what they might be planning to do to me at this very moment. I fear for my life. I am afraid to get out there on the street, for who knows where they might be hiding. When I am in my house, I look under my bed, for you can never be sure, you know ..."

"If they are looking for you, they will find you when your guard is down; when you are looking away; when you are asleep. What good is your gun then?" asked the Tao.

"I agree. That is why I have stopped going outside. I can not sleep, for who knows ..." the student trailed off.

"May be there is no one looking for you after all? May be you are not that important? Look at the world outside. People are going about their own business. Hardly anyone has time to know you, let alone kill you," the Tao said.

The student returned after three weeks. "I was so wrong, O Tao," he began.

"The lesson is over for today," said the Tao, abruptly, "The rest of the day you will self-study Book 3, Chapter 5 : 'Knowing Thyself'."

The student nodded his head, and opened to Chapter 5.

"And, oh," the Tao said, "Come and see me in the evening for some NRA detox."

Tao 1:32 - Power

"Let me tell you a story that I once heard from a friend, O Tao," said the student.

"Would love to hear it," the Tao was encouraging.

"A timid man goes to the Mosque. Before the prayers, he goes to collect a bucket to fill with water, and to wash. He finds that there is a new man in charge of the buckets. He greets the man and picks up a red bucket. The man in charge says, 'No! Not the red bucket. Take the green one.' The timid man is surprised but does as told. The next day it happens again. As he is about to pick up a yellow bucket at random, he is told, 'No. Today you take the blue bucket.' Days pass. The same story continues. Every day he bends down to pick up a bucket, and he is told to pick up a different one. One day, the timid man could take it no longer; he asks, 'Why? Why do you always ask me to pick up a bucket different from the one I choose?'…"

"Why, indeed?" the Tao was curious.

"The man in charge of the buckets says, 'Look, I am poor. There is so little in my life. This is the only place where I can order someone to do as I like. It makes me feel powerful. Please don't take it away from me.' The timid man stops asking his questions, and does as he is told. The man in charge is happy."

"Well, enough of this story nonsense!" said the Tao, "Now, all of you will complete Lesson 3 in complete silence. No talking, no whispering, no movements! I do not want any sound for the next hour while I have my siesta."

Tao 1:33 - Cricket

"I am learning to play cricket, O Tao," said the new student, "and I love it."

"What is cricket?" asked the Tao.

"Oh, it is a game where one person throws a ball, and another person tries to hit it with a bat. If you can hit it far, you get runs. If you miss, and the ball hits the stumps, you get out."

"Go on," prodded the Tao.

"There are eleven fielders who try to catch the ball, but most of the time they don't have much to do," said the student, "Oh, and did I mention, a game of cricket can last even five days."

"Five days!" exclaimed the Tao, "And so many players! Now that would be a huge loss of useful work, would it not be?"

"Well," said the student, "those players would not be good for anything else, really! But have I told you about the hundred million who stay glued to the television screens watching the game all those days?"

"No wonder nothing ever gets done!" pondered the Tao.

Tao 1:34 - Spring Break

"Welcome back, Class!" said the Tao, "It has been a long time. How was your Spring Break?"

"I spent my time on the beach, admiring my toenails and beyond," said the first student.

"I went traveling to the far corners of India in search of salvation," said the second student, "but all I found were shopping malls."

"I stayed here. It was warm, and the beer was cheap. Why go anywhere else?" said the third.

"Wonderful!" said the Tao, "As for me, I went searching for the true meaning of Spring Break. I travelled far, from Argentina all the way to Yemen, by way of Majorca. Then, in a seedy hotel called Rosalinda on the cheap side of Zanzibar, as I was jumping on it, the mattress finally died under my feet with an awful sound. Boing! I looked down, and there it was ..."

"What?" curiosity got the better of the second student.

"A broken spring."

Silence. Snigger. Sigh.

"A terrible, terrible joke," said the students, almost in unison.

"Lighten up, Class!" said the Tao, "A dash of humor never killed anyone."

Tao 1:35 - Rumors

"Rumors of my death have been greatly exaggerated," said the Tao, smiling, one Sunday morning. He was holding a book by Mark Twain.

"Why do you say that, O Tao?" asked the student.

"I heard that down in the Valley, a man is spreading rumors about me. 'The Tao is dead,' he says. I think he misses the point. Tao is not me. Tao is the Way. Tao is an idea, and I am merely a container. An idea can never die; it is like a seed that comes back to life every spring, and spreads by creating more. The Way will forever live on," said the Tao, "I think the man was confused by the black smoke from our barbecue last Wednesday. He must have thought of it as a sign of some calamity. Must remember to send up some white smoke today."

There was a collective sigh of relief in the class.

Then a hand went up. A student said, "I had been to the village bazaar the other day. I heard another man talking about you, O Tao. He called you 'mysterious'. I think someone else suggested that the up on the hill, we are involved in the dark arts of Black Magic, Voodoo, predicting future, sermonizing and some such nonsense. He is not right, O Tao, is he?"

"Rumors of my life have been greatly exaggerated," smiled the Tao.

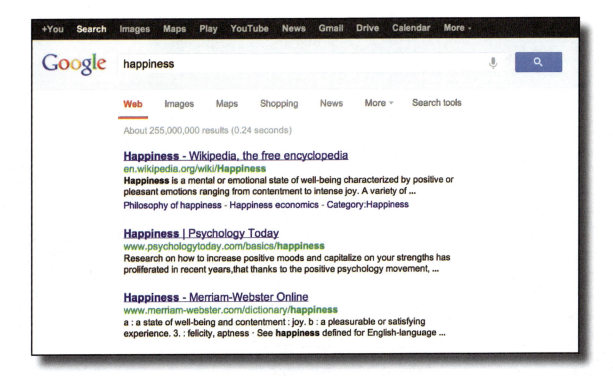

Tao 1:36 - Happiness

"I had been looking for happiness for so long, and finally I found it," announced the student one morning.

"Congratulations!" said the Tao, "May be you want to share with the class how you found the world's most elusive emotion?"

"It is not elusive anymore, O Tao," the student beamed, "It is so easy to find now. It has never been this easy in the entire human history."

"Pray, go on," said the Tao.

"Down in the Sandy Valley, they have invented this amazing presence they call the Internet. It is all-encompassing; it is even bigger than God, they say. It holds everything inside it, all the world's information, it's emotions, it's fears, it's knowledge, and even it's wisdom. It is so big that to find anything you need a monster of a machine they call the Google. The Google knows where things are stored in the cavernous belly of the Internet beast. It is the magic of this Google that found me happiness."

"Curious, I must say. And what does happiness look like?"

"Hard to say. Happiness has 255 million different forms, or so Google said. But they all seem to be adorned in the same boring colors of blue, green and black. It did not look that interesting. I know I found happiness, but I am not really happy about it," said the student.

"Perhaps happiness on the Internet is an illusion," sighed the Tao, "Only Google knows for sure."

Tao 1:37 - Birth

"What is this great deal being made about births and birthdays?" asked the student, "I think birth is such a non-event, at least for the one who is being born. Come to think of it, here I am, born and all, but I never wanted to be, played no part in it, did not know it was coming my way, and did not even know it for some four years after it actually happened! Now that all evidences point to it having happened, I can not remember a thing. It is perhaps a good thing too that I have no memories of it, for I am sure it must have been traumatic."

"It is not the birth, but what it brings to you, that is important," said the Tao.

"And what is that?"

"Life," said the Tao, "Life is such a limited time offer. Believe me, it is the greatest deal you will ever have. Use it or lose it."

"Use it I will," said the student, as he blew away all the candles on the cake in one breath.

Tao 1:38 - Death

"What is the meaning of death?" asked the student one morning, despondent.

"Death is a transition of consciousness from body to the collective," said the Tao.

"Death looks more like final to me, rather than a transition. My father has passed away, that is final; that is not a transition," said the student.

"It is final for the body, but it is a transition for the consciousness. We are part of a giant collective fabric of consciousness. Remember what I had told you about leaving behind a ripple? That ripple is what we contribute to the collective consciousness. Death liberates your consciousness from your body, to be part of that collective. At death, your body dies, but your consciousness lives on because it has permeated other consciousnesses to be forever a part of theirs. When you are alive, your ripple is given a bodily form. With death, your ripple does not need a form anymore, for it has become part of the whole, the collective," said the Tao.

"Not sure it makes me feel any better," said the student.

"Some things are hard to explain," said the Tao.

Tao 1:39 - Hope

"There is no hope for me," the student said, looking dejected.

"But there is, always," said the Tao, "One thing is certain: there is always hope."

"Not in my case," said the student, "I have become a complete nervous wreck. Listening to your pseudo-philosophical babble every day and night has killed all my interest in life. I quit."

"In that case I shall bid you adieu," said the Tao, "I hope you will be back here next year."

"Good luck with that!" said the student, leaving.

"There is always hope," smiled the Tao, "We will waive your tuition if you do come back."

"Really?"

Tao 1:40 - Light

"You have brought me from darkness to light, O Tao," said the student, "I was lost, lonely, in despair. You brought me to where I am full of hope."

"I merely showed you the light," said the Tao, "You walked into it by yourself."

Tao 1:41 - The End

"Is this the end?" asked the student.

"Yes, ... and no. Yes, it is the end of this phase of learning. No, it is not the end; it is only the beginning of next," the Tao said, "What do you plan to do now that you have begun your true learning?"

"I will travel around the world. Seek darkness of ignorance, and shine the light of knowledge upon it," said the student.

"It is easy to think of oneself as learned, and most others as ignorant, but remember that everyone has some learning, it is just different from yours. So, try to assimilate and spread knowledge; take what is good, leave what is not useful," said the Tao.

"Do you have some parting thoughts as I leave?" asked the student.

"Yes. Have you asked yourself the right question?"

"What is the right question, O Tao?"

"It is this: What are you going to do with your life to make the world a better place?"

ACKNOWLEDGEMENTS

Where do I begin? I think I will begin with the inspiration. It happened many moons ago, when I was in a haze of smoke, and to my utter disbelief, and that of those around me, I was found to be spouting what was promptly classified by my friends as pseudo-philosophical psycho-babble. It was written off as a disease that I will be cured of, and fast. But alas, that was not to be. In the years that followed, my brain was completely and irreversibly rewired, thanks to the effects of the potent hallucinogen, and the fountain of wisdom was left bubbling its pungent fumes forever. To thee I bow, O the fundament of all substances, I acknowledge your mind-bending chemistry.

A book like this would not have been possible without the explicit and implicit support of family and friends. First of all, I would like to express my tremendous gratitude to my wife, Meenakshi, for all her suggestions and support, and, most of all, patience. My son Rahul has single-handedly ensured that I stay focused on improving the quality of my photography and writing. A lot of the credit goes to my parents and to my family, who have been the rock of support and inspiration in my life.

A special thanks to my dear friends, Anurag Acharya and Madhuri Chattopadhyay, for long discussions over endless cups of tea, and for reviewing the drafts of the book and suggesting many improvements.

Most importantly, thanks to all my friends and followers on Facebook, whose appreciation and comments on the "Tao series" were the driving force for me to continue to write. They are too many to thank individually, but let me name a few in no particular order: Anu Acharya, Samanvitha Rao, Pallavi Raman, Pinaki Poddar, Roli Khattri, Aruna Nambiar, Moushumi Sen, Raghu Nambiar, Anu Singh, Swati Ray, Rupa Fritz, Meenakshi Mukerji, Rajeev Char, Surajit Sengupta, Geetha Vallabhaneni, Samiran Basak, Namrata Desai, Indra Singhal, Vinita Singhal, Shankar Srinivasan, Tejinder Singh, Anuradha Srikantan, Sowmya Simha, Lily Patil, Arup Basu, Arundhati Bhowmick, Vinee Purohit, Murli Thirumale, Meera Kaul, Sanjay Dhar, Sadhana Nadkarni, Rashmi Nayak, Sushant Dhar, Indira Iyer, Kaushik Pal, Jyoti Bhattacharjee, Prabhu Venkatesh, Kalyani Penta, Suchitra Vaidya, Kakoli Dutta. To you all, and to the many unnamed ones: you are the soul of this book; it would not have been possible without your constant encouragement.

How do I end? I think I will end with a toast to friendship. After all, what is life if not filled with friends, music, laughter and love, peppered with an occasional dose of pseudo-philosophical psycho-babble?

Made in the USA
San Bernardino, CA
01 May 2014